D0363875

AMEN AND HIS FAMILY

Joan Evans Hartman

Hartbeat Books
Ripley, Tennessee

for Sooo Jane Tice with the best of all good wishes! Joan

To

Scott, Evans, and Lane

Publisher's Acknowledgement

The publisher wishes to acknowledge and thank Lanzer's Printing in Union City, Tennessee for the generous advice and assistance in seeing this publication become a reality.

Amen And His Family

Text copyright 2012 by Joan Evans Hartman
Published by Hartbeat Books
111 Lankford Drive
Ripley, Tennessee 38063

First Edition 2012
Published and printed in the United States of America
Hartbeat Books ISBN Number: 09762515-4-X
Library of Congress Control Number: 2012900558

CONTENTS

Foreward v

Prologue 1

    William Slaton Evans … ."Amen"................................ 2

    From Practicing Law to Preaching God's Laws 4

    "Miss Helen"... 6

BREAKING BREAD.. 9

Chittlins... 11

Secong Hand Sodas and the Gifted Goat 12

Baskets For the Needy 14

The Bishop Comes to Dinner 14

Helen: Seamstress, Seer, and Chef 15

Christmas Custard and Cookies... 17

Lagnappe…A Little Something Extra 19

Eating God's Bread 20

A "Wallop" of Goat's Milk 21

Fruits of the Garden... 22

Turnip Greens.. 24

Banquet in Africa 26

GIFTS, GREAT AND SMALL.. 29

Cucumbers, A Mandolin, and One Thin Dime 31

The Gift of Work 32

The Gifts of Invitation.. 34

Cauliflower Ears, Pennies, and Progress 35

Mother's Money to Gift 36

Amazing Gifts 38

Silver and Gold.. 39

PHOTOS 41

A WAY WITH WORDS 63

Streaking Through the Circle Meeting 65

See You in the Funny Papers.. 66

Welcome to the District Superintendent 69

Quick on the Uptake 69

Shared Slacks 72

Not to Be Distracted 73

John Speaks His Need.. 74

Others in Paris Who Had a Way With Words 75

Please Sit Here With Me 78

Reassuring Words 79

Dad, the Poet... 80

Words Spoken for Senator Alben Barkley 82

EPILOGUE 87

SINE DIE 91

FOREWORD

First of all, this book is dedicated to the late Dr. and Mrs. William Slaton Evans, about whom this story is told, and to Dr. William Slaton Evans, II, the late Jimmy Mann Evans, the late Dr. John Wesley Evans, Betty Shaw Evans, Katherine Guttery Evans, and Rosemary Trevathan Evans, all of whom added to the story!

Secondly, this book is dedicated to the author's children, Scott Hartman, Evans Hartman, and Lane Hartman McKinney, and to the other Evans grandchildren: Rebecca Goodson, Rev. William Evans, III, Ellen Markwell, Elizabeth Dickerson, Jane Sharp, Lynn Johnson, Jimmy Evans, Jr., Amy Dennis, Dr. Lea Helen Evans, and Lt. Col. John Wesley Evans, Jr.

Finally, this book is dedicated to Helen and Slaton's great grandchildren, most of whom did not have the privilege to know their great grandparents or their Great Uncle Jim and their Great Uncle John:

>Ben and Carter Goodson
>Madison, Lily, and Slaton Evans
>Will, Cole, and Shaw Dickerson
>Leslie Kilzer
>Chris, Anthony, and Nikolas Markwell
>Sarah and Katie Sharp
>Katherine, Tucker, and Sam Johnson
>Jimmy and Ben Evans
>Anna, Julia, David, and John Walter Dennis
>Stephanie, Grace, Robert, and David Hartman
>Katy Shellenback

To this last group, "the torch is passed" to you to carry on the legacy of the Evans family. AMEN!

PROLOGUE

William Porter Evans (1848-1932) and Mollie McKinney Evans (1857-1924) settled in Lavinia, in the old First District of Carroll County, Tennessee. They died before many of their grandchildren knew them.

A letter written by Porter to his mother, Eliza Katherine Porter Evans, when he was a student in 1878 at Athens College (TN), gives insight into his quest for knowledge.

When Porter's 1832 copy of <u>Man in Genesis and Geology</u> was discovered in recent years by the family, there was further insight for his progeny. (In the front of the book, in Porter's handwriting, we learned that he purchased it for fifty cents on April 17, 1872 from A.B. Mills in New York City ... this ordered from a man in rural Carroll County, Tennessee.)

Porter's obituary told of his being "a leader in the affairs of the community, active in all the endeavors that go to make up community life. He joined the Methodist Church in youth and lived a life consistent with his profession."

Mollie's obituary read that "she had given her life as a living sacrifice for her companion and children." She also was described as "a good Samaritan, giving her means and time to those she could befriend." Both Mollie and Porter were long-time members of Pleasant Hill Methodist Church in Carroll County, Tennessee.

They both were descended from Patriots of the early days of the United States of America. David Porter (born about 1760 in County Antrim, Ireland), Porter's maternal great grandfather, served with General George Washington at Valley

1

Forge in the bitter winter of 1777-1778. Porter Evans' paternal great grandfather, Thomas Evans, served as a lieutenant in the North Carolina Militia from 1776-1783. Daniel Evans, Porter's grandfather, also served in the Revolutionary War. Mollie's paternal great-grandfather, William John McKinney (born 1729 in Scotland, died in 1785), also served in 1781 in the Revolutionary War.

Mollie and Porter were parents of these children: Mable Evans Manning, Jennie Lee Evans Byerly, Henry Bascom Evans, Benjamin Franklin Evans, Arthur Exum Evans, and William Slaton Evans.

William Slaton Evans …"Amen"

William Slaton Evans was born in 1901 to Porter and Mollie Evans. It seems that his older sister, Jennie Lee, ruled his life to the point that she told him what clothes he would wear and when he would wear them! (See section of photographs.)

When Porter went to Jackson, TN to take his sweet potatoes to sell and to "look in" on his investments at the National Bank of Commerce, he stayed at the livery stable. When he returned to the family home, Slaton was treated to the cheese his "Pap" had bought and stored in his pocket … especially for his youngest child.

Dad's brothers Bascom and Frank often took the roles of making their younger brother's life difficult. Each of them recounted the story of their mother's missing eggs. Since the profit from selling butter and eggs was her money, she hoped that the cows and hens would produce well.

When Mollie was missing the estimated number of eggs, she believed that the hens were nesting in the field. She offered Slaton a nickel if he found the missing nests and eggs. Slaton's diligent search led to smoke rising from a boiling pot in the field. Much to his surprise, Bascom and Frank were having a huge egg boil!

As Slaton raced to the house to tell what he had found, Bascom and Frank took a short-cut and wrote in the sand of the creek bank: YOU HAD BETTER COME BACK!

Slaton said that it was weeks before he left the porch and his mother's side! He only could imagine what his older brothers would do to him, since he discovered the missing eggs and the boiling pot!

Their life in rural Carroll County, Tennessee was fairly uneventful. Dad told of riding a mule to a nearby cross-road when they heard there was an automobile there. Since he had never seen one, he was sorely disappointed to find only a gypsy wagon.

Once Porter brought home a bicycle, which he had purchased for only fifty cents. Although the bike had no chain or pedals, the boys could ride the bike down the hill in front of the house.

After you read of Porter Evans' quest for knowledge, it would follow that education was important for his children. When it came time for the boys to attend high school, they were sent to McLemoresville, Tennessee to live with "Cousin Luther" McKinney and to attend McLemoresville Collegiate Institute. One of the teachers there, Miss Bertie Harvey, later would become the wife of Bascom Evans, the elder brother of Slaton.

From the Practice of Law to Preaching God's Laws

Slaton had the desire to study law. He enrolled in Cumberland University School of Law in Lebanon, Tennessee, where he graduated in 1926.

Judge J.T. Peeler in Huntingdon, Tennessee, offered Slaton a position with his law firm. We are told that Slaton earned a favorable reputation, practicing as a young attorney and scheduled to inherit the lucrative law firm from the soon-to-retire Judge.

In 1927 Slaton married Helen Mann, of McKenzie, Tennessee. It was while they were members of the Huntingdon Methodist Church and working with the youth in the Epworth League that Slaton felt the call into the ministry.

Bascom Evans told that he had assisted his younger brother with financial support, while Slaton attended law school. When Slaton told his brother that God had called him into the ministry, Bascom queried: "Just how BADLY do you believe that God is calling you?" Slaton's response: "I had rather preach the Gospel of Jesus Christ than to sit on the Supreme Court of the land." Our cousin Marjorie Gossett recalls that her dad, Frank, told of replying : "Then you'd damn well better do it!"

It was back to school for Slaton, this time at Vanderbilt Divinity School in Nashville. This was the height of the Great Depression. Times were hard, Helen was now pregnant with their first child, and she was working as cashier in the old Wesley Hall cafeteria.

When the bishop called to ask if Slaton was interested in becoming the pastor of the Gleason, Tennessee Methodist Church, Slaton didn't hesitate to accept this call.

After a short time at Gleason, Slaton became the pastor of the Malesus, Tennessee Methodist Church. The proximity of this church enabled Slaton to enroll at Jackson, Tennessee's Lambuth College, where he graduated in 1932.

The Lambuth Lantern, the school annual of that year, relates the following information about his years there:

> Mr. Evans is the first student in the history of Lambuth to fill the office of president of the student body for two years. And we believe he deserves this honor, for during the period from '30 to '32 affairs of the college have been capably managed and have been settled in a just, impartial manner.
>
> Perhaps Mr. Evans deserves more credit than we ordinarily assign him, for at the same time he was conducting our student affairs he was attending to duties as head of a family, pastor of a church, and was officer in various other local organizations.

During the years at Lambuth, Slaton served as pitcher on the college's baseball team, where he was given the nickname of "Shotgun" by the catcher on the baseball team. Dad threw underhanded with his knuckles, sometimes touching the ground in his pitching delivery. The catcher said that, when Dad turned loose his pitch, no one knew exactly where it would land. It kind of scattered like a shotgun shell!

Slaton's grandson, Jimmy Evans, Jr., now has in his possession one of the baseballs used by "Shotgun" during his pitching career at Lambuth.

Lambuth always was dear to Slaton's and Helen's hearts. All four of their children and five of their grandchildren graduated from Lambuth. Slaton was a long-time member of the Lambuth Board of Trustees and served as both secretary and president of that board. Slaton was the recipient of the first of Lambuth's honorary doctorates. An endowed scholarship at Lambuth was established in their honor by their children.

After student days at Lambuth, Slaton was in the full-time Methodist ministry. It was the first grandchild, Becky, who gave Slaton the name he became known by all of his grandchildren... ."Amen."

"Miss Helen"

The daughter of Howard Lee Mann (1867-1942) and Florence Thompson Mann (1873-1965), Helen Mann was born in 1901. Howard Mann was a farmer and a teacher at "singing schools." In their later years he and Florence operated a boarding house in McKenzie, Tennessee.

(Years later their grandson Bill Evans recalls that he could smell MaMa Mann's apple pies she had prepared for dinner that day the minute the family stepped out of the car for a visit with their grandparents!)

"Miss Helen" served as one of the teachers of Carroll County's two-room Terry School. She boarded at the home of Mr. and Mrs. Joe Parker and Mr. and Mrs. Jim Parker.

The Parkers told "Miss Helen" about a young attorney in Huntingdon, Tennessee. One Sunday afternoon they invited Slaton Evans to call on "Miss Helen." Before he arrived another young man, NOT INVITED, came to call.

When Slaton arrived and saw the other young man, he met "Miss Helen" ...and went straight out the back door!

This unauspicious introduction led to box suppers, where

Slaton was careful to bid on "Miss Helen's" boxes. When he tasted her caramel tarts, he became even MORE interested in her, he told his children in later years.

"Miss Helen" had a thumb that naturally turned back toward the other hand. He observed this. When the ladies at the party stood behind a sheet and extended their hands for young men to choose their partners, Slaton chose "Miss Helen." She wondered how he knew it was her hand!

Their marriage took place on June 15, 1927 at the home of her parents in McKenzie. The <u>McKenzie Banner</u> featured an account of the wedding:

EVANS - MANN WEDDING

LOVELY HOME AFFAIR
Popular Carroll County Young People
Are United in Bonds of Wedlock

William Slaton Evans of Huntingdon and Miss Helen Mann of McKenzie were married last Wednesday afternoon at three o'clock in the home of the bride's parents, Mr. and Mrs. Lee Mann in McKenzie in the presence of a number of special friends of the contracting parties. An impressive ring ceremony was said by the Reverend C. L. Smith of Huntingdon.

The Mann home was artistically decorated in a white and pink color scheme, the improvised altar making a beautiful setting for the marriage.

The bride and her maid, Miss Charlotte McNeill of McKenzie, were beautifully gowned in pink flat crepe, and the bride carried a shower bouquet.

The bridal couple left that afternoon, motoring to Bruceton, where they took the train for a bridal trip to Nashville and Chattanooga.

(Helen, upon celebrating their 60th wedding anniversary, told her granddaughters that their "bridal trip" was the equivalent of one to Europe in the girls' day!)

To this marriage were born William Slaton Evans II (born 1929), Jimmy Mann Evans (1932-1992), Joan Evans (Hartman) (born 1935), and John Wesley Evans (1938-2003).

(After the death of Howard Mann, MaMa Mann ceased to operate the boarding house. She spent the last twelve winters of her life with Helen's family. During those winters she pieced beautiful quilts, many of which are now owned by her grandchildren and great-grandchildren. When she sold her quilts, she gave a portion of the money to her church, Shiloh Cumberland Presbyterian Church in Carroll County, Tennessee.) (See photo)

BREAKING BREAD

"Chittlins" *

Our Dad had a great fondness for chittlins! He told the story of Jim's birth in July, 1932 in Jackson, Tennessee. Dr. George Brasher, the grandfather of our good friend Dr. George Brasher, III of Temple, Texas, delivered Jim at the parsonage of Highland Heights Methodist Church in Jackson.

Dr. Brasher and his wife Irene returned the next day to check on Mother and Jim. Daddy had taken this opportunity to build a fire in the backyard of the parsonage and cook what he aptly called "a mess of chittlins."

Dr. Brasher, also an aficionado of chittlins, noted Dad's activity and the distinct aroma coming from the backyard. "Are you cooking chittlins, Brother Evans?" he asked. Dad told him that he was and asked Dr. Brasher if he would like to join him for lunch. So the good Doctor and Dad sat down together for one of their favorite meals.

When Dad retired from the active ministry in 1970, he and Mother chose to reside where at least one of their children was permanently located. Dad was elated to find other chittlin eaters in Dyersburg, Tennessee.

Soon after Dad's first chittlin meal in Dyersburg, he was called to sit on the jury. Since Dad had experienced an earlier time as an attorney in Huntingdon, Tennessee, he was looking forward to a time on the other side of the bar.

The morning of jury selection Dad eagerly went to the Dyer County Courthouse. Only a short time later he returned home to Mother's puzzlement. She asked, "Why are you back so

---

* For readers not from the South: "Chittlins" are the intestines of pigs used for food.

soon?" Dad, too, was puzzled about why he was dismissed by the Honorable Watkins Ewell.

Dad surmised that it was for one of three reasons: (1) He had been an attorney and perhaps he would be too hard on those to appear before the judge. (2) He was a retired minister and perhaps would be too "easy" on the ones to appear in court. (3) He had been seen eating chittlins at the local cafe!

Second Hand Sodas and the Gifted Goat

Life in Gibson, Tennessee, was an idyllic one ...so much that, after five years there, Mother, Dad, Bill, and Jim cried on the way to the new appointment in Memphis. In the midst of tears, Bill recalls that Jim said, "Daddy, when I am grown, I'm going to get married, move back to Gibson, and stay 'til the Judgment Day." He loved Gibson. We all did.

Although there were few diversions in Gibson, Bill and Jim created their own. (Mother told of their playing postmen with the love letters found in the attic!)

While Dad was by Joan's side, as she lay critically ill in the Methodist Hospital in Memphis, Bill and Jim were "busy" back in Gibson. They made their way to James Atkins' grocery there in Gibson and discovered stacks of empty cold drinks outside the store.

Some of the RC Cola, NuGrape, and Orange Crush bottles still had small amounts of the drinks that "whoever" had not finished. Bill and Jim proceeded to have a party with the remaining amounts of the soft drinks!

When they returned home, Mother inquired about where Bill

and Jim had been. After initial denial about being "downtown," Jim confessed the visit to Mr. Atkins' grocery.

Mother got a bottle of castor oil, gave Bill half of it and Jim the other half. The memory of the "after effects" was so vivid that it was YEARS before the boys would accept an offered drink of cola!

During the Gibson years the late Brown Parker brought a goat to the parsonage for Bill and Jim. For reasons unknown, "Rastus" took a strong dislike for Jim.

One day Rastus cornered Jim in the parsonage hen house. Jim grabbed Rastus' horns and pushed the goat as far as his strength would allow. Rastus responded with fury and repeatedly butted Jim. Bill was amused, until Dad saw what was happening. He ran off Rastus and "took Bill to the woodshed" for not helping Jim AND for enjoying it.

Mother called Brown Parker and told him that he would have to come and get the goat.

A few days later Brown returned with what Mother described as "some of the nicest looking meat you could imagine."

At dinner that evening Jim asked, "Is that Rastus?" "Yes," Mother said.

No one ate a bite. Dinner was over.

Baskets for the Needy

There was a time when Methodist preachers in West Tennessee and West Kentucky moved to their new appointments in November.

Katherine Evans recalls the story of one of the Evans' November moves. Soon after the Evans family moved to the new church, a committee was meeting in regard to Thanksgiving baskets for the needy.

One of the ladies on the committee spoke and said, "I don't know who they are; but I have been noticing a lady with four small children in our church services. They look like they might appreciate one of the baskets."

"Amen," immediately knowing that the lady was referring to his family, said, "I'm sure that they would."

Can you imagine how embarrassed the lady must have been, when she learned that the lady with the four children was the new parsonage family??!!

The Bishop Comes to Dinner

Mother was well known for her excellent cooking. She could pack lunches to cause envy of those who surveyed the contents.

Bill Evans III is the only grandchild who spent an entire summer with "Amen" and "Granny." He tells that his co-workers' eyes were on his sacks, as he eagerly tore into his wax paper wrapped surprises.

Likewise, Mother could prepare a delicious dinner for twenty or so. When Bishop Watkins and his Cabinet came to dinner in Paris, Tennessee, it truly was a meal to remember.

Ten year old John Wesley, known for his antics, was instructed to be on his best behavior. There came a lull in the conversation, and John posed a question to the bishop. "You know," said John, "you can tell a lot about a person by the piece of chicken he eats." "How so?" asked the bishop.

John proceeded to say that a drummer would choose a "drum stick," and a flier would choose a wing. "Guess what a dead-end kid would choose?" John asked the bishop. All of the diners were amused …except our Mother!

Actually, the bishop was charmed by John. After dinner the bishop took John aside, told John that he had something for him, and that it would be arriving soon.

A few days later a bust of the first John Wesley was delivered. In a note the bishop told that the bust had been purchased in Edinburgh, Scotland, when he studied there. It was waiting for just the right person.

Helen …Seamstress, Seer, and Chef

Helen was a multi-talented lady. She was a self-taught seamstress who made beautiful clothes for her family and herself …even clothes for the boys from pieces of Dad's outgrown or worn garments.

No one could have described Helen as extravagant …except for her hats. Jane Evans Sharp, one of Helen's grandchildren, remembers Helen being "stylish with her hats."

On one shopping excursion Helen never batted an eye, as

she told the sales lady, "I will take ALL THREE of them." (At least one of them was a Mr. John hat, which was the epitome of style at that time!)

Elizabeth Evans Dickerson and Dr. Lea Helen Evans, two of Helen's granddaughters now occasionally wear some of these hats.

Perhaps Helen's family most remember her delicious meals. Our mouths water when we think about those summertime dinners she prepared ...butterbeans, fried corn, pickled beets, and sliced tomatoes from Dad's garden ...always with her delicious corn bread and, often, peaches with her angel food cake.

Judy Hazlewood, one of our cousins, through the years has served "Aunt Helen's Chicken."

Mother even had a remedy for her inquisitive child who was afraid of chickens. She would lay a chicken feather in the drawers which were "off-limits" to the child!

Mother had an unusual perception. She would announce to Dad that one of their grandchildren was sick. Sure enough, when she called, she learned that their grandson Evans Hartman was so sick that the doctor was calling each day to check on him.

Weeks before Dad learned that he was to have surgery for cancer, Mother dreamed that Dad was at the back door. When she answered the knock at the door, there stood Dad ... not saying a word, but with three giant tears on his face. She pondered that dream and understood it, when Dad learned that he was to undergo surgery.

Christmas Custard and Cookies

In the many parsonages where we lived there always was a delicious Christmas dinner. When we were young these dinners were shared with Dad's brothers and their families: Uncle Bascom, Aunt Bertie, Jean and Judy; Uncle Frank, Aunt Gladys, William Edward, and Marjorie.

During one time at Christmas Mother was bed-fast with the shingles. We children selfishly worried that we wouldn't have our traditional Christmas dinner. "Not to worry," said Dad. That man, remarkable in so many ways, prepared our traditional Christmas dinner …all by himself.

Dad inquired about the location of Mother's recipe for home-made rolls. He found the wrong recipe …the one she used for large quantities. We had rolls for Christmas dinner and for many days to follow!

It didn't matter what we had for Christmas dinner, if we had Mother's custard. She insisted that it was not <u>boiled</u> custard. "It is <u>cooked</u> custard," she insisted. There were brown sugar cookies for the children in the family.

Betty Evans, Bill's wife, has inherited the assignment of making the custard. Lane McKinney, "Amen" and "Granny's" granddaughter, inherited making the cookies for the "children of all ages" in the family. In the last years of "Granny's" life she gave Betty and Lane the recipes and passed along those responsibilities. Lane tells of throwing away several "batches" of cookies before the cookies resembled those of "Granny."

Recipe of Custard

"Cooked Custard Recipe"

1 gal. whole milk
4¾ cups sugar
4 rounded tablespoons flour
   pinch of salt
12 large eggs

1 pt. of milk
1¼ cups sugar
1 rounded tbsp.
   pinch of salt flour
3 large eggs

Beat eggs in mixer till foamy, then add sugar that has been mixed with flour and salt gradually. Then beat till well blended, set aside.

Put milk in large size container and set in pan of hot water on stove and double boil milk till you can see a skim on top of milk, then gradually stir in egg mixture and cook custard till it begins to thicken and will coat the spoon (stir custard as it cooks) This takes time.

Take off stone and stir in 12 whole cloves then strain custard and cloves through sieve into another large container and add 3 tablespoons vanilla and set aside to cool. (I put ice cubes in cool water in my sink and set container of custard in sink to cool) When cool put in large jar and place in refrigerator. I think custard is much better made 2 days before serving it as it has time to mellow.

Whip ½ pt. of XX cream and stir into custard before serving it. We also like a dash of nutmeg at eating.

Lagnappe ...A little Something Extra

There usually was something "extra" to enhance Mother's meals. Cucumber slices and onion rings in vinegar complimented the summer vegetables from Dad's prolific gardens.

Our young neighbor, "Little Kenny" Clayton, was born shortly after we moved to Paris, Tennessee. He often was a guest at our table. His grandfather, Mr. Bradsher, was a retired railroad man. So, when Mother offered the cucumber and onions to Kenny one day at lunch, he said, "No, thank you, I am a retired man from cucumber and onions."

Mother's home-made sweet pickles were a welcome "side." (Dad almost killed all of us, when he purchased the wrong kind of lime for adding crispness to the pickles!)

There always was a cruet of pepper sauce on the table. Dad liked to add this to his turnip greens.

A summer-time "extra" for the iced tea was a small pitcher of grape juice. When John's wife Rosemary came for one of her first visits, she spied the bread on the table and the pitcher of grape juice.

Surprised she was when Rosemary discovered we were not celebrating Holy Communion at the table, as she guessed we would!

When Bill enrolled as a freshman at Lambuth College, he came home thirteen weekends in a row. Then Dad told him not to come home for a month. He felt that Bill needed to become involved in campus life.

Mother made the best devil's food cakes. At the end of one of the weekends when Bill came home, Bill took back one of those cakes to Lambuth. He shared the cake with his roommate each night at 10 o'clock, and it was hidden under the bed until the next night.

Mother and Dad claimed that the late Memphis Doctor Tom Mitchell had saved the author's life as a young child. Therefore, at Christmas he and the many doctors to follow in our lives were the recipients of Mother's cakes and banana nut breads.

A little "extra" for them, too.

Eating God's Bread

Mother and Dad were of the opinion that their children should not participate in Holy Communion, until they understood what they were doing. (Do we as adults fully understand the significance of this service?)

At this point Bill and Jim were regulars at the Lord's Table. John and Joan were eager to gather at the altar with the others and to partake!

The parsonage at that time was next door to the Highland Heights/Memphis Church. One Sunday afternoon John suggested that he and Joan should go over to the church and take Communion.

Little did they know that the bread would be so tasteless! Also, they were not considering the consequences of eating ALL of the bread and drinking ALL of the grape juice.

Just before the evening service and the offering of Holy Communion to those unable to attend the morning service, Dad came running over to the parsonage. "Do you know anything about the communion elements?" he asked Mother. Of course, she knew nothing about these necessities for the observance of the Lord's Supper.

One look at the "tell tell" purple rings around John's and Joan's mouths answered Dad's question!

The next time when Holy Communion was served, John and Joan were among those who gathered at the Lord's Table.

A "Wallop" of Goat's Milk

Often in pretty weather the family would take a Sunday afternoon ride. As Bill got older, he sometimes was allowed to be the chauffeur.

Since we lived in Memphis at the time and since Dad remembered that the Misses Angel lived in the country and had invited us to drop by for a visit, their home became our destination that day.

The maiden ladies seemed glad that our family and Joan's friend, Betty Walker, had come for a visit. It was a hot summer day in the days before air conditioning, and Miss Angel announced that it would be nice to have something cool to drink.

We children envisioned tall glasses of lemonade …or, even better, bottles of cold carbonated beverages which we rarely enjoyed!

You can only imagine our dismay when the ladies brought forth a tall pitcher of GOAT'S MILK and the appropriate number of glasses!

Miss Angel first poured glasses for Dad and Mother …and then to the children and Joan's guest.

We all watched Dad as he took the first sip. His countenance told us children that the milk was not well received!

21

Miss Angel also noted Dad's reluctance and suggested that the flavor would be enhanced by a "wallop" around in one's mouth.

We children intently watched Dad as he "wallopped" the milk. When Dad announced that the "wallop" didn't seem to make the milk any tastier, he placed the glass on the side table …and we children knew that we were "home free"!

Miss Angel wisely observed that goat's milk required a cultivated taste, and she brought out the welcomed pitcher of lemonade!

So much for the "wallop" of goat's milk!

Fruits of the Garden

It was fortunate, indeed, that "Amen" enjoyed gardening. Had this not have been one of his pleasures, "Amen's" family would not have fared so well …especially during the Great Depression.

Many summer days "Amen" would harvest a bushel of butterbeans and admonish the children that they would need to help Mother shell the beans. None of the children seemed to have objected …except John, then ten or eleven years old.

He would shell for a few minutes and then tell Mother that this activity made him NERVOUS. In fact, he told her that shelling made him "feel like he was up against a brick wall." This ploy worked! Mother excused him. The rest of us children wondered why we didn't think of that!

We were grown before we learned that John had to clean the bathroom during those shelling times!

In his retirement "Amen's" gardening was expanded. "Amen" announced to Helen that he thought he would plow up their backyard and plant a big garden. When he went to his back yard shop, Helen called Jim to tell him of "Amen's" plans.

Soon Jim "dropped by" the house to offer a plot for a garden out of town near the home of the late Alvin and Ava Hall. It was there that the fenced garden produced tomatoes, green beans, squash, beets, butterbeans, potatoes and onions …a bountiful garden without any sign of weeds.

At the suggestion of Ray Ashley, for the first time "Amen" grew asparagus in the smaller backyard garden. He also tried Jerusalem artichokes. A grape arbor, thornless blackberries, and apple and apricot trees brought joy to many of the family, neighbors, and friends.

"Amen" had read of a method of growing tomatoes whereby a plastic gallon jug was buried beside the plant. Perforations were made in the bottom of the jug. Both water and fertilizer were given the plant through the mouth of the jug. Jane Evans Sharp, one of the granddaughters of Helen and "Amen," remembers that this plant in the backyard garden grew to over six feet tall. "Amen" kept a total of the tomatoes harvested from that plant. It gave them hundreds of tomatoes to enjoy! (See photo)

Turnip Greens

In his retirement "Amen" established a small rose garden for Helen. It was surrounded by a concrete edge to keep the lawn grass from invading this special space, which she could enjoy from the kitchen window.

It was "Amen's" pleasure to go to the garden early in the morning and to gather roses for Helen to enjoy.

When "Amen" was unable to have his big garden, he decided that the space around the roses would be an ideal place for greens to grow. Without consulting Helen, he broadcast turnip and mustard seeds in the bed of roses.

One morning some days later Helen was working at the kitchen sink and noticed "greenery" among the rose bushes. As she questioned "Amen", he admitted that this was wasted space where he thought their favorite greens might grow.

At first, Helen thought that the greens distracted from the roses. At harvest time, however, she was pleased that a "mess" of greens was only a few steps away from the kitchen!

One fall "Amen" was hospitalized in Tupelo, MS, where John practiced medicine. When Joan called to inquire if there was anything that she could do, "Amen" told her that she could plant some greens in the rose garden. This was one job which she had never done, and, naturally, Joan was apprehensive about doing this.

"Amen" advised: "Go to the shed in the back yard and look in the freezer. There you will find both turnip and mustard seeds. On the lower shelf of my work bench you will find a salt shaker. Fill it with a tablespoon of each of those seeds, and place tape over half of the holes of the shaker. You will then be ready to sow the seeds."

He further directed Joan to rake over the soil of the rose bed, to broadcast the seeds, and to water lightly the space. Joan proceeded to follow the directions, not knowing that she didn't have to sow ALL of the seeds in the shaker!

Needless to say, an ABUNDANCE of greens graced the rose bed, when "Amen" returned home! In fact, he then requested that Joan "thin out" the greens!

As Jim observed Joan's first planting, he told her: "Now, Joan, our parents 'hire' me from the shoulders up and you from the shoulders down!"

Jim's last job was as Commissioner of Transportation for the Sate of Tennessee. Prior to that he was president of Pioneer Contracting Company in Dyersburg, TN. He instructed those who were preparing medians on highways to take special care in seeding those spots.

One of those men to where this work was assigned told that he carefully followed Jim's directions. When Jim went to inspect the seeding of this particular spot, he reached in his pocket and scattered some seed himself ...those of turnips!

Some days later he accompanied the original sower to the spot. "If I didn't know better," Jim said, "I would think that these were turnip greens growing here."

The original sower was perplexed! "Why, Mr. Jimmy, I oversaw this personally, and absoluterly there were no greens sown," he said.

Jim then had to admit to his prank

25

Banquet in Africa

Bill served for many years on the United Methodist Church's Board of Global Ministries. It was in this capacity that he attended a meeting of the World Council of Churches in Nairobi, Kenya.

Those in charge of the conference assigned pastors in attendance to preach in various city churches. When Bill and some of his minister friends heard of these plans, they declined the invitations. Instead, it was the wish of Bill and his colleagues to rent a car and to seek out a small church out in the Kenyan country.

Not knowing where the men would be at lunch time, Bill and the other men asked the hotel food service to prepare box lunches for them. These boxes were filled with the fried chicken and sandwiches of picnic-style fare.

Off the ministers went in their rental car out to the unknown countryside. When they reached the first church, the men stopped to worship with the local folks.

Although Bill recalls not being able to understand some of the service, the visitors were able to join in singing of familiar hymns.

After the service, they were welcomed warmly by the congregation, and the pastor's wife invited the men to join her family for lunch. Bill replied that he and his friends had brought box lunches with them and that they would be happy to add those to the meal which she had prepared.

Since the pastor's children had never seen box lunches, they were thrilled to have them! Bill and his colleagues proceeded to eat the lunch the pastor's wife had prepared.

At the end of the meal Bill inquired about the meat they had eaten. When the pastor's wife told them that they had eaten MONKEY, Bill was grateful that he didn't know what he was eating at the time!

GIFTS GREAT AND SMALL

Cucumbers, A Mandolin, and One Thin Dime!

Our family has been the recipient of many gifts, all appreciated. ...some more than others!

There was the neighbor boy in Jackson, Tennessee who "gifted" Bill by painting his new Buster Brown shoes GREEN! Bill rather liked the new color, but the boy's mother insisted on replacing the shoes.

Bill was invited to preach the Memorial Sermon at the Memphis Annual Conference of the Methodist church. He related this story at that time: "I remember one time when a knock came on the parsonage door. When it was opened we were greeted by a church member who said, 'These cucumbers are too big for us to eat. We thought you all might use them.' How big were they? Big enough that when you squeezed them they felt like a sponge. We were taught in all things to give thanks, and we did. We thanked God that we didn't have to eat them! And into the garbage they went."

Bill recalled another call from a church member, who inquired if the parsonage family liked chicken. "I guess we did," Bill said, "because that's about all the meat we ever ate." The church member came and left two chickens tied at the feet, hanging over the clothesline! "And we thanked God again," Bill said, "and started looking for somebody to get those chickens ready to cook."

Two ladies brought a mandolin to the parsonage. None of us knew how to play it, but we seemed to have enjoyed plunking on it at all hours.

One day we returned from school, and it had disappeared. When we inquired about it, Mother said: "The music is GONE!" We decided that she had heard enough of our "playing."

Dad was asked to marry a couple at the Madison County, Tennessee Fair. At the end of the ceremony, the groom inquired: "How much do I owe you?" Dad jested, "Oh, just whatever you think that she is worth!"

The groom reached in his pocket and handed the preacher a DIME. Dad said that it was all he could do to keep from giving the groom a nickel and saying, "Here's your change!"

The Gift of Work

Even though Jim ran away from school on the second day of school in his early years, he became the consummate business man.

He approached Mr. E. W. Smith after church services one Sunday evening at St. Paul Methodist Church in Memphis. Jim suggested that Mr. Smith might need a boy on Saturdays at the hardware store to run errands, to go to the post office, and to sweep the store.

Actually, Mr. Smith told Jim that he had been thinking about hiring someone for that kind of work. Jim was hired.

With his earnings Jim began what became a lifetime of sharing what he had with others. He never came home on Saturday night unless he brought John and Joan, his younger siblings, little gifts …a pack of chewing gum, a bar of candy, or a trinket from the store.

This first employment led to others: delivering early morning newspapers, loading fuel on barges, and serving as head resident at his dormitory at Vanderbilt, to name a few. Jim became an attorney-at-law and, finally, the Commissioner of Transportation for the State of Tennessee in the cabinet of Governor Ned Ray McWherter.

Bill also had, as Mother said, "a mind to work." Bill remembers the odd jobs he did for spending money when he was a young boy …collecting Coke bottles (3 cents each) and coat hangers (1 cent each), selling calendars ($1.00 each), and mowing yards (from $5.00 to $10.00).

He asked Bell Telephone Company for their scrap lead, which he melted and poured into molds …and sold back to the company for 25 cents a mold!

Bill's four-year newspaper route with the Memphis Commercial-Appeal brought him enough income to purchase a new baseball glove. (Bill hit three home runs in one baseball game and set a high school record that, to our knowledge, has been tied but not broken.)

(Bill played in a regional high school game at Memphis' old Russwood Park, where the player of the game was to be selected to be sent to New York to play at Yankee Stadium. After Bill's home run record of the previous game, he KNEW he would be selected …only to strike out three times and for the pitcher of the game to be selected. To add insult to his bruised ego, his hard-earned glove was stolen!) These initial enterprises led to others: working for the Paris, TN Public Utility Company; serving as a student pastor on the Whiteville, TN Methodist Circuit while he was a senior at Lambuth College; selling ties at an Atlanta downtown men's store while he was a student at Emory University; serving pastorates in many West Tennessee churches, as a United Methodist district superintendent, as the Administrative Assistant to Bishops Ernest Newman and Kenneth Carder, and finally in his "retirement" as pastor of the

Enville and Holly Springs United Methodist Churches in West Tennessee.

John had his share of summertime jobs and the ability to "make a deal" wherever he was. This talent led him to serving as a "go-between" with his friend the jeweler. He sold many engagement rings to his fellow medical school students and assorted jewelry and silver goblets to some of the doctors under whom he trained.

Bill has and John had the same gift of sharing with others that Jim possessed.

The Gifts of Invitation

Our family was invited into homes to share meals. Sometimes Mother and Dad would accept those invitations, while we children were in school. Such were the times when Mother and Dad dined in Paris, Tennessee with the daughter-in-law and granddaughter of Tennessee's Governor James Porter in his historic home.

During revival meeting times the entire family would visit in homes. At one of those times John was playing with a rabbit before lunch. To secure the pet while we were having lunch, John "hid" the rabbit under the bedspread of our hostess.

While we were having lunch, out of the corner of her eye, our hostess, Mrs. Mary Phillips, noticed something strange. There was movement under her bedspread!

The rabbit was relocated …and John went home with a pet rabbit!

One of the loveliest Sunday dinners after church was in the home of Dr. and Mrs. Horton Dubard in Memphis. They were a young, newly married couple.

Mrs. Dubard had set a beautiful table, with her recently acquired linen, china, and silver. Although at this time John and Joan were young children, this gracious lady entrusted them with her silver goblets!

Brain research tells us that we best remember events where our senses are involved. Doubtless it is because of this that we remember, even now, this beautiful setting and the dinner that included roast beef and rice.

Cauliflower Ears, Pennies and "Progress"

Children notice anything unusual. On the family's first Sunday at Highland Heights Church in Memphis, the family was seated on the third pew from the front. A man and his wife were seated in front of us.

Jim was quick to notice the "cauliflower" ears of the man in front of the family. "Bill," Jim said, "Look at that man's ears!" The man heard him, and his ears seemed to turn pink! Jim THEN observed, "And they light up, too!"

After the service the man turned and aksed, "Which of you boys was talking about my ears?" They replied by pointing to each other!

Mrs. Allie Brattain, who was raised as an Episcopalian, distinguished herself by the way she worshipped in the Methodist Church …by kneeling for prayer at her pew during the services.

Even more than by the way she worshipped did she distinguish herself. She knew how to make happy parsonage children!

Often she inquired if Joan might like to accompany her to the MOAT, Memphis Open Air Theater. It was there that Joan was introduced to the world of light opera...and a lifetime love of music.

All year long Mrs. Brattain saved her pennies in a cloth sack. When Christmas came one year, here came Mrs. Brattain, bearing the sack ...for John and Joan!

Countless hours were spent counting those pennies, rolling them in papers to carry to the bank for paper money, and discussing how this treasure would be spent.

It still makes us sad to drive by the site of Mrs. Brattain's beautiful home on Summer Avenue in Memphis. Long ago the home of that dear lady was razed to allow for "progress" along that busy thoroughfare.

Although her home is gone, Allie Brattain lives in our hearts.

Mother's Money to Gift

As a young child Mother was known to be responsible and business-like. She told of hiding under her bed to practice her letters and numbers, because she had to get away from her younger sisters to do this.

This seriousness about life led Lynn Evans Johnson, one of Mother's granddaughters, to ask, "Was Granny ever young?"

Dad never charged for officiating at the many weddings and funerals over the years. However, the grooms and families of the deceased almost always gave him some kind of gift.

Once, when Dad married a couple at Highland Heights

Methodist Church in Memphis, the groom gave Dad a pair of leather gloves. Dad placed them in a drawer for safe keeping.

A good while later Dad tried on the gloves, only to discover a $10.00 bill in each finger and thumb of the gloves! Dad said that he actually had considered giving away the gloves, before he made this discovery!

Just as Dad's mother Molly had her "butter and egg" money, Helen was the recipient of Dad's honoraria. Business-like as Helen was, she invested this money.

When it came time to move from Memphis to Paris, Tennessee, Dad shared with Mother his concern about money to make that move. "Not to worry," Mother said, as she made plans to withdraw funds from "her account."

As Dad and Mother were about to retire in 1970 to Dyersburg, Tennessee, Dad once again shared concern about funds. Since they always had resided in furnished parsonages, there would be items to purchase. They would need a washing machine, dryer, refrigerator, freezer, and furniture.

Once again Mother withdrew from "her account" to give the necessary money.

Thankfully, expenditures for relocation of ministers to their new appointments in the Memphis Annual Conference is now the responsibility of local churches.

Amazing Gifts

"Amen's" cardiologist concluded that what "Amen's" parents described as "growing pains" were, more than likely, misdiagnosed. It was the cardiologist's opinion that "Amen" probably had rheumatic fever when he was a young boy.

As a young man in his forties "Amen" experienced problems with his heart and was bedfast for several weeks.

When "Amen" was a hearty fifty-five year old man, he suffered a severe attack of kidney stones. In that time in the fifties no lithotriptor had been discovered. The result of this attack was the removal of one of "Amen's" kidneys.

Nothing prepared the family, however, in 1965, when it was discovered that "Amen" had cancer and would have to undergo major surgery.

While "Amen" was hospitalized for several weeks, one of his parishioners sent a gorgeous arrangement of roses EACH DAY. How they brightened his spirits!

As generous as this gift was, it paled in comparison to a call "Amen's" daughter, Joan, received.

Lynn Watlington, whom Joan had met but was not well-acquainted, made a memorable phone call to Joan.

"Joan," she said, "this is Lynn Watlington. I have talked with God about your Dad, and He gave me this message. Your Dad will not only survive this surgery, but God has told me that He has much more work for your Dad to do, and he will live a long life. It has been good to talk with you."

It was during this time that John, "Amen's" and Helen's youngest son, was involved in his training as a medical doctor.

When Joan related to John the phone call from Lynn, his reply was, "She hasn't been to medical school."

Indeed, Lynn's prophetic call came true! "Amen" lived another thirty-six years of a life that influenced countless others.

One such life who was influenced by "Amen" was expressed in a letter sent by Mary Lib Hayes to the author after "Amen's" death:

> My good intentions have failed me again, but I do want you to know how saddened I was to hear of Dr. Evans' passing. Of all the ministers I've ever worked with or had as my pastor, he stood out as the "Good Shepherd" and I shall always be grateful for the confidence and faith he showed in me when he asked me to join the church staff.

Silver and Gold

On the occasion of "Amen's" appointment as superintendent of the Paris, Tennessee, district of the Methodist Church, the good people of Highland Heights Church in Memphis presented "Amen" and Helen with an extremely generous gift. How surprised they were when they opened a chest of sterling silver flatware ...service for twelve!

When Helen and "Amen" celebrated their fiftieth wedding anniversary in June, 1977, parishioners from every charge he had served through the years gathered in Dyersburg, TN to offer their congratulations.

Originally, Helen and Slaton had discouraged the family from planning such an event. Rather, they felt that a family dinner would be sufficient.

The family prevailed. Afterwards, the happy couple declared that it had been one of the happiest days of their lives.

As one of their dear friends, the late W. V. Fortner, passed through the receiving line, he pressed two gold coins in Helen's hands and two gold coins in Slaton's hands.

A golden tribute for a golden friendship!

William Porter Evans and Mollie McKinney Evans

The Evans Barn
(Commissioned by Dr. and Mrs. D.M. Gossett)
(Painted by Elizabeth Ellison)

William Slaton Evans ("Amen") as a child

The Evans Brothers

(l - r) **Henry Bascom Evans, William Slaton Evans ("Amen"),
Benjamin Franklin Evans**

"Amen's" graduation picture from Cumberland Law School

MaMa Mann

Helen Mann Evans' engagement photograph

Bill and Jim with Rastus

"Amen" and his prize tomato plant *(top)* **and with Helen's roses**

49

"Amen" and Helen before Easter Sunday at
Broadway Methodist Church, Paducah, Kentucky

Eulogy From American's Neighbors

PADUCAH, Ky.—Thousands of people, the great and small of Kentucky and surrounding states, gather in the street in front of the Broadway Methodist church as the casket bearing the body of Sen. Alben W. Barkley is lifted from the hearse and taken into the church for brief services. —Staff photos by Joe Rudis

Nashville Tennessean

"Amen" on right front

51

Portrait of "Amen" by Paul Penczner

Portrait of Helen by Paul Penczner

Helen and "Amen" at First Presbyterian Church
in Dyersburg, Tennessee

"Amen" and Helen's 50th Anniversary Photograph

Bill and Betty Evans' 50th Anniversary

(Front, l-r) **Madison Evans, Lily Evans, Carter Goodson, Slaton Evans;** *(2nd Row, l-r)* **Wes Goodson, Becky Goodson, Ben Goodson, Cole Dickerson, Shaw Dickerson, Bill Evans, Betty Evans, Will Dickerson, Leslie Kilzer,** *(Back l-r)* **Dana Evans, Bill Evans, III, Elizabeth Dickerson, Bill Dickerson, Ken Markwell, Ellen Markwell, Chris Markwell, Sarah Markwell, Anthony Markwell, Nikolas Markwell**

Jim Evans Family

(Front Row)
Jim Evans and Katherine Evans

(Back Row, l-r)
**Amy Evans Dennis, Lynn Evans Johnson,
Jimmy Evans, Jr., Jane Evans Sharp**

**Jim Evans and sign on Highway 412
in West Tennessee, named for him**

Joan Evans' Family

(Front Row, l-r) **Katy Shellenback, Lane McKinney**

(Back Row, l-r) **Kim Hartman, Scott Hartman, holding Mary Grace Hartman, Joan Hartman, Evans Hartman, "Mac" McKinney**

John Evans' Family

(Front Row, l-r) **Lt. Col. John Wesley Evans, Jr., Dr. John Wesley Evans**

(Back Row, l-r) **Allison Evans, Lea Helen Evans, Rosemary Evans**

Rev. Shirley Lynn Assists Dr. Wm. S. Evans, II
at Lane and "Mac" McKinney's wedding

A WAY WITH WORDS

Streaking Through the Circle Meeting
and Playing Postman

Days in Gibson, Tennessee produced a number of stories that have been passed down in the family.

On this day Mother was to entertain the ladies of the church at a circle meeting. She took Bill and Jim aside and explained that the ladies were coming to the parsonage and that they MUST be on their best behavior. They were sent outside to play.

Bill wondered what would make the visit a memorable one for the ladies. He told Jim that he thought that they should pull off their clothes, run through the room where the meeting was to be held, and jump on the sofa.

Although Jim was the younger of the two boys, he told Bill that he didn't think that this would be a good idea. Bill assured Jim that this would be fun!

The ladies assembled for the meeting, and Bill and Jim proceeded to get ready for their part of the meeting.

As the meeting got underway, Bill and Jim positioned themselves in the doorway of the living room. Bill told Jim, "I'm right behind you!" Jim took off on his run, landed in the middle of that sofa, threw his arms up as high as he could reach, and hollered "Whee!" Instead of following Jim, according to the plan, Bill picked up his clothes and retreated to the back porch.

Many years later the boys declared that THEY had invented "streaking"!

Obviously, there was not much to do in Gibson to entertain two little boys. So they had to "make" their fun.

Bill and Jim were rummaging in the attic of the parsonage and came across some letters tied with a ribbon. Bill suggested that they might play postman with the letters. Off they went, leaving letters behind doors all over Gibson.

When they returned home, Mother asked what they had been doing. Bill told of finding letters in the attic with a ribbon and their playing postman.

Mother said, "Run as fast as you can and get all of those letters!"

That night when the children were all in bed asleep, Mother and Dad built a bonfire in the back yard and burned the letters …actually, only the ones retrieved!

See You In the Funny Papers!

This was the name Dad gave to one of his sermons. He saw the reflection of human nature and humor within the comic strips.

One of Dad's favorites was "Hambone's Meditations," which appeared regularly in Memphis' The Commercial-Appeal. One of the all-time best was Hambone's observation about a preacher: "He's done quit preaching and gone to meddlin'!"

Dad had a great sense of humor. He only had a fringe of hair at the nape of his neck. And, yet, he made regular visits to the barber shop! Once he asked the barber why he charged the same price as for those who had a full head of hair. The barber explained, "We charge you first to find it!"

On one of those visits the barber, knowing that one of the men present was a member of a church that refrained from using musical instruments in their worship services, posed a question to Dad. "Where in the Bible does it say that you can't use an organ in church?" the barber asked.

Dad, knowing full well what the barber was seeking to do, said, "It's over there just before the passage that says that you should use a pitch pipe to 'heist' the tune!"

Soon after Dad and Mother retired to Dyersburg, the members of the Presbyterian Church there lost their pastor. They asked if Dad would agree to "fill in," until they could find a pastor from within their denomination. Dad agreed. Our family thought that the church members didn't seem to be in a hurry, since he was there for nine months! Dad and Mother made some wonderful friends there at First Presbyterian Church. (See photo)

On his final Sunday as their pastor, he observed that the congregation had asked him to marry their young people, to baptize their babies, and to bury their dead; but they had not trusted him with the wine! (He later learned that an ordained Presbyterian was required to serve communion in the church.)

Two of Mollie Evans' best friends were Jennie and Slaton Johns. When Dad was born, he was named for his "Uncle Slaton" Johns. As a birth gift, they gave Dad a five dollar gold piece and told Grandmother Evans that he was not to spend it but to keep it.

When Dad was a young boy, he wanted to buy a calf and raise it. His Mother asked how he intended to pay for it, and Dad told her that he would use his gold piece. She reminded him of her promise to "Uncle Slaton" and "Aunt Jennie." Instead, she would lend Dad the money, and he could repay her when he sold the calf.

Years later Dad had our friend the late Les Hays, a well known jeweler, to make a necklace with the gold coin. Mother wore that necklace with pride.

Still even many years later, when Mother was no longer wearing the necklace, she asked Dad to bring it to her so she could give it to Amy, Katherine's and Jim's youngest child, who is the only grandchild Mother and Dad saw from birth until she left home to go to college.

As Amy was given the necklace, she asked: "What am I going to tell my sisters about your giving this to ME?" To this, Dad quickly replied, "Why, you can tell them that you found it as you were walking in the woods!"

All of Slaton's children inherited his sense of humor and being quick on the uptake. Jim offered the observation that one of the ladies in the choir at the Highland Heights Church in Memphis must have a beautiful voice. Jim's friend asked how he knew without hearing her sing, to which Jim replied, "Haven't you noticed her bird legs?"

One day Dad's district superintendent, Dr. C.C. Grimes, called on the phone. Bill answered and spoke to Dad in the best way he could mimic Dad's "boss." "It's your BIG BOSS, DR. C. C. GRIMES!" Dad was relieved to hear Dr. Grimes' chuckle.

Welcome to the District Superintendent!

When "Amen" served as district superintendent of the Memphis District, the pastor of the church where the Evans family worshipped one Sunday had overlooked Dad's presence.

As the offering was taken to the chancel, one of the ushers passed a note to the pastor telling him that his superintendent was present.

The pastor declared, "I am delighted to see Mrs. Evans and Dr. Evans, who is the father of most of their children." Actually, what he meant to say was that he wanted to welcome Mrs. Evans, Dr. Evans, and most of their children!

After the service this pastor quickly sought out Mother to offer his deepest apologies to her. Mother, in her gracious way, said, "Brother _____, everyone here who knows us knows that my husband is the father of all of our children. Don't worry about it."

Incidentally, this is the same pastor who, in a later service, directed the congregation to "Please notice the new dossal cloth hanging to my rear."

Quick On the Uptake

Perhaps it was because Dad had been an attorney and had to be convincing in the court room. Perhaps it was the Bachelor of Oratory he earned at Cumberland University School of Law along with the LL.B. Those who were privileged to hear him preach believe it was because he truly was called into the ministry.

Always quick on the uptake, Dad used this to great advantage. Our Dad was bald almost all of his adult life. On an occasion in Booneville, MS he was introduced by a man who claimed that there was a town in Arkansas named after Dad …Bald Knob! Dad quickly retorted that there was a town in West Tennessee named after the man who introduced him …Hollow Rock!

Bill Evans II inherited this talent. On his 80th birthday nine of his family surprised him by being at the Enville, TN United Methodist Church for worship service.

The lady who presided over the service that day observed that, when Bill died, they should bury him as the Archbishop of Canterbury had been buried …under the altar. Quick on the uptake like our Dad, Bill said, "That will be fine if you will come to see me every Sunday!"

In the Methodist churches of the Memphis Conference until the 1960's it was the custom for pastors to live in furnished parsonages. These parsonages varied as the one in Malesus, TN (where Helen told of feeding the chickens through cracks in the floor) to the one at Trinity Methodist Church in Memphis. It was there that one of the church members, Mr. Ray Evans (not related to our family) built the nicest parsonage which the Evanses would inhabit …the patio here built around a 100 year old oak tree.

As we moved to a new church and a new parsonage, Mother did her best to turn the parsonage into our home. This included flower boxes on the front porches, flowers in the yards, and slipcovers over ugly sofas.

As we moved to this particular parsonage, Mother inquired as to how long it had been since the interior of the parsonage had been painted. Her research led to the information that it had been several years since that work had been done ….about ten, the parishioners thought.

Mother called together the parsonage committee …all men. She proceeded to cite the work that was needed, first of all the interior painting.

She then said that she felt that there should be new draperies in the living and dining rooms. To this, one of the men on the committee went over to one of the drapes, pulled it away from the window, and observed, "I don't see any holes in these drapes." Mother quickly asked, " Do you wait until you have holes in your trousers to buy new ones?" He said, "BUY THE DRAPES!"

Jim shared this quick uptake with Mother. When he moved to Montgomery, AL to practice law, Mother inquired about his provision for room and board. Jim stated what his plans were for a room. Mother was quick to ask about his plans for meals. Jim said, "I'm going to have a mistress, and she will provide my meals."

Just as quick as he was, Mother said, " Now, Jim, you be careful. Not every girl can cook!"

Mother left this earth without our knowing FOR SURE if she understood what Jim had said. We tend to think that she fully understood!

John had a "saltiness" with his way with words. In fact, Mother told him that his language would be a "stumbling block." (Somehow, that never happened.)

Several years ago Joan had surgery in Tupelo, Mississippi, where John was a urologist. Joan left the hospital and spent five delightful weeks with John and Rosemary. When Joan's friend Mary Scott called to inquire about Joan, Mary asked John if she might speak with Joan. "She's out on her paper route now, but I will have her call you when she comes back, " John said.

Donna Overstreet also called. "How is Joan?" she asked. "Oh, Donna, have you not heard? Joan has _____ (a terminal disease)" John replied. Donna began to sob, and John quickly said, "Oh, hell, Donna, Joan's fine!"

Even at an early age, the Evans twins, Elizabeth and Ellen, had a way with words. When their Granny and "Amen" came to visit, they asked if their grandparents had any money for them. The girls indicated that they didn't want any of that "round kind." They wanted some of "that long green kind."

Shared Slacks

Slaton's and Helen's children were grown before they realized they had grown up poor! (This also was true of many who grew up during the Great Depression.) Sam Levinson entitled his autobiography Everything But Money. This was us!

During this time Dad recalled that very little money "passed over his palm." And, yet, we prospered …with Dad's abundant garden, a cow on loan, chickens at the parsonage, and an occasional ham gifted to us.

Years later, when Bill and Jim were at Lambuth College, they wanted some of the popular gray flannel slacks. They pooled their money and bought one pair, to be shared.

At that time Jim was "seeing" a young lady who was a hostess for the GM&O Railroad. One evening Jim met the train in Jackson, Tennessee and rode with her some miles down the road.

As Jim and "the hostess" alit from the train, another suitor of "the hostess" greeted them. Jim and the suitor got into what might be called a fracus.

When Jim returned to Lambuth, he told Bill what had happened. Bill's question was NOT about Jim's well-being but "Are our slacks damaged?"

Not To Be Distracted

Dad had been invited to preach the Homecoming service at his boyhood church, Pleasant Hill in Carroll County, Tennessee.

It was one of those times that Mother was unable to go with Dad that Sunday. So Dad took their oldest child, Bill, with him.

Bill, a small boy at the time, was told by Dad to sit on the front pew and hold Dad's hat for him during the service. One of the ladies at the church took it upon herself to look after Bill.

Not liking this arrangement, Bill ran to the pulpit while Dad was preaching and stationed himself behind Dad's legs.

Never missing a beat, Dad preached the entire sermon with Bill clinging to his legs.

Another time Dad was well into his sermon when he was interrupted. A gentleman, seated at the front of the church, became overcome by the power of the message.

The man rose, turned toward the congregation, and chanted: "Listen to him, brothers, he's telling you the truth! Listen to him, brothers, he's telling you the truth! Listen to him, brothers, he's telling you the truth!" Each time the man's words became louder than the previous ones!

Of course, this momentarily distracted Dad from his sermon! However, he said that it taught him a great lesson: Always have an outline in front of him!

John Speaks His Need

When the family lived in Paris, Tennessee, ten year old John developed appendicitis. It soon became apparent that he would need an appendectomy.

At that time, the late 1940's, there was no hospital in Paris, only the Rhea Clinic where John's surgery was performed.

After the surgery John was recuperating at the Clinic. Since this was a fairly small place, there was a limited number of rooms for the patients.

John was placed in the room with a lady who was in labor. Her moans were disturbing to John, and he asked the nurse to move him.

The nurse explained that there was no other room available. She could move him out in the hall. John agreed to this arrangement.

The moans of the expectant mother continue to bother John. While the nurse was making her rounds, John took the matter into his own hands. John wrapped the sheet around him and proceeded to walk home, some three blocks away from the Clinic.

The nurse was mortified when she couldn't find John! She had looked everywhere, when she decided that she had to call our house and notify our parents.

"Not to worry," Mother said. John had walked home and was asleep in his own bed.

Somehow, we preacher's kids seemed able to adjust to most any situation, to speak our needs, and even to check ourselves out of the hospital, if necessary!

Others In Paris Who Had Ways With Words

Growing up on Lee Street in Paris, Tennessee was an idyllic life. We walked to town, when ever we had the notion or the need. No doors were locked. There was always something interesting to do, when we finished our chores.

Miss Johnnie Looney, a maiden lady who was in her late 80's or 90's (Who knew?), was one of our neighbors. She often sat on the porch of the house where she took room and board. As we children passed on the way to school or to town, she spoke to us of her needs: "Tell your mother that it has been a while since I had any turnip greens."

Dad told Miss Johnnie that he was going to her home church for a meeting and that he would be glad for her to accompany him. True Victorian lady that she was, Miss Johnnie thanked him and said that it would not be good for Dad to be seen with a woman other than his wife.

Joan graduated from playing with dolls to playing with a "real live" baby, "Little" Kenny Clayton. He was born in January, after the family moved to Paris. Many were the times, when he was old enough, that he joined the family for meals at our table. Foods that Mother served, Kenny would enjoy …even though we were told that he rejected some of them at home!

It was at one of these times when Kenny was a guest at the Evans' table that he posed this question to our mother: "Do you know what a balanced diet is?" Mother advised Kenny that she, indeed, had a good idea what that included. Then she asked Kenny what HE thought was a balanced diet. He quickly answered: "A root and a fruit, a meat and a sweet, and a pickle to tickle"!

One of the "perks" of being a "preacher's kid" in Paris was going to the Capital Theater there and only paying the tax on the ticket for the movie! (Of course, the movie had to have a "G" rating in the <u>Parent's Magazine</u> for Mother to allow us to go!)

Kenny loved to accompany us to the movies. He offered the observation that we could "save time" if he ate lunch with us before we left for the featured attraction! What a little guy he was to have such a way with words!

Suzie Fitzsimmons and Harriet Wheatley were right there on Lee Street for Monopoly, Rook, and Canasta. Carolyn Brisendine often came over from across town to play. In the summer we took picnic lunches with us to Ogburn Park to play tennis under the tutelage of Miss Lamar Roberts.

In the evenings Jim and some of the older boys joined us for "Kick the Can" right there on the street, since there was very little traffic on Lee Street or the intersecting Crawford Avenue. When we tired of this, we turned to "Hide and Seek." We remember that those evenings were about the only times other than meal times that we saw our Mother resting. She seemed to take pleasure in seeing and hearing the neighborhood children play.

John had his playmates, Larry and Ronnie McGehee, right down on Crawford Avenue. The McGehee garage was the site of Ronnie's and John's poker games, about which we are quite sure that our parents never knew!

Larry, later to become the chancellor of the University of Tennessee at Martin, special assistant to the president of the University of Tennessee at Knoxville, and vice-president of Wofford College, was The One who best described the Paris we knew. For many years he wrote a column, "Southern Seen," for many newspapers in Alabama, Georgia, Kentucky, Mississippi, North Carolina, South Carolina, Tennessee, and Virginia.

The late Dr. McGehee perfectly described Lee Street in the chapter entitled "Neighborhoods" in his 2005 book, Southern Seen:

> This is the time of the year when I most miss Lee Street. Actually, there are several streets tied together in that memory lane, but Lee Street was a center artery for the Lee Street Gang, our version of the Little Rascals and Our Gang back in the 1940's.
>
> Susie, Harriet, Billy. Buzzy, John, Joan, Ronnie, and I were at the core, but occasionally we let in the younger ones like Cindy and Mary Ann, or the older ones like Alan and Jim, or the ones from three or more blocks away like Joe, Andy, Bailey, Ralph, and Paul ...especially when we needed baseball teams in the summer, sleds for Peden Hill in the winter, or Indians for us cowboys to shoot and hog-tie in the spring.
>
> Ah, innocence! Ah, neighborhoods! What could Eden have had that Lee Street didn't? In the photo albums of our minds, the survivors, it is still there: good as it ever was and better.

What a way with words he had!

Please Sit Here With Me

Some of the kindest words Mother ever spoke were offered to the Reverend Shirley Lynn.

It is the custom for the ministers' wives of the Memphis Annual Conference to gather for a luncheon during the time of the Annual Conference. On this occasion Shirley Lynn was attending the luncheon for the first time as a minister's wife.

You can imagine that Shirley was a bit apprehensive about this event, which was held at the Irvin Cobb Hotel in Paducah, Kentucky. Shirley had given considerable thought as to what she would wear, especially the hat that was expected to be worn.

As Shirley approached the formal dining room of the hotel that day, she realized that she had entered the front of the room. Then she saw the room already crowded with the ladies in attendance. "Where will I sit?" she wondered.

About that time Mother saw Shirley, extended her hand, and said, "Please sit with me." It was only after Shirley accepted Mother's invitation that she realized she was seated at the head table, not only with Mother but also with the bishop's wife and other dignitaries.

Many years later Shirley Lynn became an ordained minister. One of Mother's granddaughters, Lane Hartman McKinney, heard Reverend Lynn relate this kindness in a sermon she preached at Christ United Methodist Church in Memphis.

Reverend Shirley Lynn assisted our brother, Dr. William S. Evans, II, at the wedding of Mother and Dad's granddaughter, Lane McKinney, and her husband William Douthitt McKinney, Jr. (See photo section.)

Reassuring Words

Countless times in Slaton's ministry he was called on to offer words of encouragement to those facing surgery, to the bereaved, to those going off to war, and to those facing other difficult times in their lives. Helen also was called on for these words.

Many times during the ages there have been those who predicted that the world soon was coming to an end. One of these times was in the 1940's.

The lady called the parsonage and was very distressed. Her husband was a commercial pilot and was out of the city on his assigned schedule. She and their children were at home, and she didn't want them to be by themselves when the world came to the end.

She asked Mother if she thought that the prediction was going to come true. Mother told the lady that this prediction had been made many times through the ages, and she didn't believe that it was going to happen at that time.

The lady was not convinced that Mother was correct. She asked if she and the children might come to the parsonage and spend the night with us.

Now there we were, the six of our family with four beds among us and, of course, no spare bedroom. In her typical manner, Mother told her to bring the children and come to the parsonage.

The writer is not certain if the evening meal was shared. We do remember, however, the living room floor covered with pallets of quilts and blankets for the children of our family and the pilot's children. Great fun it was!

When morning came and we were all still alive, the pilot's wife was satisfied to take her family home again.

Dad, the Poet

In Dad's study were numerous books of poetry. He loved to read, write, and memorize poetry. Scott Hartman, one of Dad's grandsons, found this poem in Dad's writing in his Mother's old coffee bean grinder:

> There's a scene that brings my whole life back,
> As cold and faint I rove;
> It's my Mother's Sunday coffee
> By the old kitchen stove.

Dad rarely gave our Mother a gift without enclosing a poem he had written. She said that she had rather have the poem than the gift!

As a surprise to Mother one Christmas Day, Dad gathered a collection of poems he had written for her. Betty and Bill Evans commissioned a calligrapher to copy the poems and bind them in a book. We are quite certain that this was one of Mother's favorite gifts of all her life. From the time she received it, the book lay beside her chair …so that she could read from it whenever she chose.

This is the first poem in the book, written for Christmas, 1952, the Christmas before Mother and Dad's first grandchild, Becky, was born. (The gift was a piece of luggage.)

o Mother dear,
With all good cheer,
This gift to you I bring;
'Tis Christmas time
So this little rhyme
Right now to you I'll sing.

This gift is small
But in it all
The things you'll need you can carry;
If a trip you plan
Without your "man"
You will not have to worry.

Don't turn away
With brief survey
And think there's nothing in it,
For I am true
When I tell you
My love is packed up in it.

And children, too,
Hear all of you!
This story I'm unraveling;
Come a baby small
With its tiny call
And "Grandma" will be traveling.

Words Spoken for Senator Alben Barkley

When Dad served as the pastor of Broadway United Methodist Church in Paducah, Kentucky, his best known parishioner was former Vice-President of the United States and then Senator Alben Barkley.

Many times Dad was invited to give the invocation, when the beloved Kentucky Senator spoke. The last time this occurred, Dad observed to Senator Barkley that he often had offered a prayer for "The Veep", as he was affectionately called, before he spoke. Dad suggested that the Senator might come to church and offer a prayer before Dad spoke. The Senator agreed.

This was the last time Dad saw Senator Barkley. While Dad was serving as a delegate to the General Conference of the United Methodist Church in Minneapolis in May, 1956, he was called back to Paducah to preach the funeral of Senator Barkley.

The church was filled for Senator Barkley's funeral. An account from the May 4, 1956 edition of the Nashville Tennessean reported thousands gathered in the street in front of the church, President Harry Truman, the former president with whom Barkley served as Vice-President, sat beside the Senator's wife. The three leading candidates for the Democratic presidential nomination, Sen. Estes Kefauver of Tennessee, Gov. Adlai Stevenson of Illinois, and Gov. Avril Harriman of New York, were in the congregation, as were twenty-four other U.S. Senators.

The Tennessean quoted the prayer offered by Dad that day: "We thank Thee for him who loved mankind, for his loyalty and friendship, his service to country ...who could walk with kings and not lose the common touch."

In the Congressional Record of the Eighty-fourth Congress, Second Session Dad's entire funeral sermon is printed:

MEMORIAL ADDRESSES

Mr. CLEMENTS. Mr. President, I have a record of the services at the Broadway Methodist Church at Paducah, Ky., last Thursday. They were conducted by the Reverend William S. Evans, pastor of the church. I ask unanimous consent that the text of the services be printed in the Record.

There being no objection, the text was ordered to be printed in the Record, as follows:

Dr. EVANS. I shall read the 23d Psalm:

"The Lord is my shepherd; I shall not want.
"He maketh me to lie down in green pastures; He leadeth me beside the still waters.
"He restoreth my soul: He leadeth me in the paths of righteousness for His name's sake.
"Yea, though I walk through the valley of the shadow of death, I will fear no evil: for Thou art with me; Thy rod and Thy staff they comfort me.
"Thou preparest a table before me in the presence of mine enemies: Thou anointest my head with oil; my cup runneth over.
"Surely goodness and mercy shall follow me all the days of my life: and I will dwell in the house of the Lord forever."

I now read John 14: 1–4:

"Let not your heart be troubled: ye believe in God, believe also in me.
"In my Father's house are many mansions: if it were not so, I would have told you.
"And if I go and prepare a place for you, I will come again, and receive you unto myself; that where I am, there ye may be also.
"And whither I go ye know, and the way ye know."

It would be presumptuous on my part to undertake to eulogize such a person as the Honorable ALBEN W. BARKLEY. He needs no eulogy. His life has been one long testimony of his faith and convictions. However, I would not be faithful to the many multiplied thousands of friends who are here in this sanctuary and who are at this moment turning their thoughts and minds toward this service, did I not give some word of appreciation. There was something inherent in his life that make all want to do him honor. It stirs the hearts of all of us to think of one who came from humble surroundings and who rose through hard work and persistent zeal to stand as one of the most honored men in our

[18]

83

Nation. He was one who won and kept the confidence of men of all walks of life, and who received expressions of that confidence as he was placed in many places of responsibility and leadership.

When news of his passing reached me at the general conference of our church in Minneapolis, Minn., I asked the privilege of that world gathering that we might stand in a moment of silent tribute to the life of this great man.

Certainly a part of the life story of Mr. BARKLEY would be found in the character of his parents. But, also, much resided within his own life. He had a vision of something big. He had a determination to pay the price to achieve greatness. He had a willingness to follow on. To my way of thinking, one of the secrets of success of life is expressed in the words of Kipling, who, as he undertook to give the measurements of man, said,

> "If you can walk with kings
> Nor lose the common touch."

Mr. BARKLEY certainly had that quality in his life. Across his beloved State and throughout the Nation and the world men have loved him, respected his integrity, followed his counsel, and have been enriched by his personality.

Many honors came to him, but no honor was greater than the sincere appreciation and high esteem in which he is held by those that knew him best. Today, as he comes back to rest in the soil of his beloved State, many, many people will rise up to call him blessed and thank God for having been privileged to be his friend.

In this service we would lift up to you some words that might strengthen our lives for the facing of this hour and the living of these days. One of the ancient men of God expressed a conviction that held him, and which I think will hold us. He said, "The Eeternal God is thy refuge, and underneath are the everlasting arms."

As we pass through shadows and carry our loads of grief, may we be strengthened by knowing that the Eeternal God is good. As he was revealed in Christ, His sympathy, love, and compassion reached out to those in sorrow. And in our times of sorrow and suffering we can be comforted by the fact that God cares. God cares because He loves us. In one of their Psalms, the ancient people of Zion sang, "I had fainted unless I had believed to see the goodness of the Lord in the land of the living." You can't read the great 23d Psalm without realizing that God is good. He is there pictured as the Great Shepherd who, though we "Walk

[19]

through the valley of the shadow of death," He will be with us. Whittier said:

"Yet, in the maddening maze of things
And tossed by storm and flood,
To one fixed trust my spirit clings;
I know that God is good."

"The Eternal God is thy refuge, and underneath are the everlasting arms." (Deuteronomy 33: 27.)

God is also great. His arms have never failed. The refuge that is offered in Him covers our needs. "His grace is sufficient." Those who have trusted Him, those who have talked with Him, those who have tested Him have found that His promises are true and that His word never fails. So, as we walk and as we live we can lean our lives upon God, who is great.

"As the marsh hen builds on the watery sod
I will build me a nest on the greatness of God;
I will fly in the greatness of God as the marsh hen flies,
In the freedom that fills all the space 'twixt the earth and the skies.
By so many roots as the marsh grass sends into the sod,
I will heartily lay me a hold on the greatness of God."

When you begin to read your Bible, you find that "In the beginning, God," and when you read the description of the last Hallelujah Chorus, you find that God is from everlasting to everlasting. He truly has been "Our dwelling place in all generations." The Eternal God that is our refuge does not change with the changing seasons. He is not ruled by the rulers of darkness. And he is not defeated by the experience of death. When you begin to think of the things that will live and last, you immediately begin to realize that these are characteristics of God: Beauty, purity of heart, nobleness of character—they never die. Truth may be ignored, assailed, crushed to earth, trampled upon, yet truth lives. Beauty also lives. Tertulian once said, "If I give you a rose, you won't doubt God any more." Beauty is of God. We are told that knowledge will pass away, but love will abide. In our time of greatest need, the love of the Eternal is most wonderfully kind.

I am simply saying that, as we rest our lives in the Eternal God, we have laid hold upon something that is eternal. In Him we live, move, and have our being. In Him we live forever. I am reminded of the last words that fell from the lips of Mr. BARKLEY:

"I would rather be a servant in the House of the Lord than sit in the seat of the mighty."

[20]

As we give our lives in service to the good and noble things, we find a life for ourselves that lives. And in Christ we can have the assurance of a life that never dies. It was said of one of the great characters in the Old Testament: "David, after he had served his own generation, by the will of God, fell asleep and was laid unto his fathers." In this faith we, too, may live.

Mr. CLEMENTS. Mr. President, I ask unanimous consent to have printed in the Record a significant telegram which was forwarded to our Senate Chaplain, Rev. Frederick Brown Harris, by Mr. W. P. Kennedy, president of the Brotherhood of Railroad Trainmen, as an expression of genuine regret over the great loss which has been suffered in the passing of our beloved colleague and courageous statesman, the Honorable ALBEN W. BARKLEY.

There being no objection, the telegram was ordered to be printed in the Record, as follows:

CLEVELAND, OHIO, *May 1, 1956.*

Rev. FREDERICK BROWN HARRIS,
    The Westchester, Washington, D. C.:
Members of the Brotherhood of Railroad Trainmen throughout the land are deeply grieved over the untimely loss of Senator BARKLEY. He was our friend. He fought for our rights when we had few friends. In all public offices held he was always ready, anxious, and willing to serve his fellow men. The millions who love and cherish decency, dignity, and honesty in government will join in mourning the loss of this great American, our beloved Senator BARKLEY.

W. P. KENNEDY, *President.*

Mr. CLEMENTS. Mr. President, many fine editorials have been written about the life of ALBEN BARKLEY, and many of them will be placed in the Record by other Members of the Senate. At this time I ask unanimous consent to have printed in the Record editorials published in the Lexington Herald, the Owensboro Messenger and Inquirer, and the Louisville Courier-Journal.

[21]

Doubtless, these words Dad chose for Senator Barkley's eulogy were heard and read by more people than any others Dad spoke at any one time in his lifetime.

EPILOGUE

Dad faithfully served forty three and one half years in the active ministry. Although Mother was not an ordained minister, she served as faithfully as did Dad.

He served the following United Methodist pastorates:

Gleason (TN) Circuit
Malesus and Medon (TN)
Highland Heights in Jackson (TN) (then St. Andrew)
Gibson and Pleasant Hill (TN) (now Grace Church in
    Humboldt,TN)
Chelsea Avenue in Memphis (now Reed Memorial)
St. Paul in Memphis
Highland Heights in Memphis
Broadway in Paducah, KY
Trinity in Memphis

He also served as District Superintendent in Paris, TN and Memphis, TN. Perhaps some of his greatest accomplishments were the seven churches he was instrumental in establishing, one in Gibson County, TN, one in Fayette County, TN, and five in Memphis, Tennessee. This is a record in the Memphis Annual Conference, perhaps in all conferences of the United Methodist Church.

After forty three and one half years in the active ministry, Slaton and Helen retired in 1970 to Dyersburg, Tennessee. Soon after they retired, the First Presbyterian Church in Dyersburg asked him to serve as their minister, while they conducted a search for a Presbyterian minister. The family felt that the church wasn't in a hurry to find a replacement, because Dad happily served there for nine months! (See photo)

Slaton's and Helen's oldest son Bill followed in his Dad's footsteps to become a United Methodist minister and later to become a District Superintendent and administrative assistant to Bishops Ernest Newman and Kenneth Carder.

Bill graduated from Lambuth College (later Lambuth University). He received the Bachelor of Divinity from Emory University and the Doctor of Divinity from Lambuth.

He married Betty Shaw from Atlanta. Their children are: Rebecca Evans Goodson - Longmont, CO; The Reverend William S. Evans, III - Severna Park, MD; Elizabeth Evans Dickerson - Dyersburg, TN; and Ellen Evans Markwell - Germantown, TN. (See Photo)

Slaton's and Helen's son, Jimmy Mann Evans, graduated from Lambuth College and received his law degree from Vanderbilt University. Jim married Katherine Guttery from Dyersburg, TN, where he practiced law with Barret and Ray Ashley and was the president of Pioneer Construction Company. He became Commissioner of Transportation for the State of Tennessee and served in that position until his death in 1992. Jim declared that it was named State Highway 412 for him. (See photos)

Katherine and Jim's children are: Jane Evans Sharp - Nashville, TN; Lynn Evans Johnson - Nashville,TN; Jimmy Mann Evans, Jr. - Nashville, TN; and Amy Evans Dennis, Oxford, MS. (See photo)

Joan Evans Hartman graduated from Lambuth College, received the Master of Arts in Education from Peabody/ Vanderbilt and the Doctor of Education from Memphis State University. She enjoyed a career as a teacher, an educational administrator, and, in her retirement, as an author of two children's books.

Joan's children are: Scott Hartman - Ripley,TN; Evans Hartman - Cordova,TN; and Lane Hartman McKinney - Collierville, TN. (See photo)

John Wesley Evans, Slaton's and Helen's youngest child, graduated from Lambuth and received the Doctor of Medicine from the University of Tennessee in Memphis. He married Rosemary Trevathan from Gleason, TN.

After serving in the United States Air Force, John became a practicing urologist in Tupelo, MS. He died there in 2003. Rosemary's and John's children are: Dr. Lea Helen Evans - Nashville, TN and Lt. Col. John Wesley Evans - Alexandria, VA. (Scc photo)

These grandchildren of Helen and Slaton are in the fields of accounting, business, dental hygiene, homemaking, marketing, the military, ministry, physical therapy, sales, speech pathology, teaching, and volunteering in their churches and communities.

SINE DIE

Years before "Amen" and Mother died, he had asked one of his beloved former associates, the Reverend Bob J. Moore, to "preach their funerals."

On April 22, 1993 Reverend Moore offered the eulogy at "Amen's" funeral. At this service Reverend Moore offered these thoughts:

"There are few people you meet in life that are truly unforgettable. Some are unforgettable because they are unique persons. Their uniqueness and strength of character leave an indelible impression upon you. Some people are unforgettable because of a relationship you had with them that was so special, so influential that they remain ever memorable. Dr. Evans was unforgettable in both of these ways."

In the eulogy Reverend Moore recalled "Amen's" influence and impact on the Memphis Annual Conference. "He was one of the giants of this Annual Conference. When he rose to speak on the floor of the conference, you listened." Rev. Moore recalled how "Amen" had led delegations to the General Conferences and Southeast Jurisdictional Conferences of the church. Rev. Moore stated: "Many feel that his stirring speech on the floor of the General Conference saved the Jurisdictional Conference structure and the election of bishops in the Jurisdiction.

He also offered these words: "Someone has said that our lives are our funeral eulogy. How right that person was. Dr. Evans' life, his ministry, and his relationships have spoken profoundly about the quality and significance of his life. His life has spoken for him far more eloquently than any of us could say today."

"He was a very self-confident person; but, at the same time he was humble. Although he was honored that his beloved Lambuth College had bestowed upon him its first Doctor of Divinity degree, he did not make a big deal about it. In fact, I never heard him refer to himself as Dr. Evans but always Brother Evans. He told me one time that a Doctor of Divinity was 'like a pig's tail. It didn't offer any meat but put a little flourish on the end."

Finally, Reverend Moore commented on the nickname, "Amen," given to Dad by his oldest grandchild, Becky, when she was young. "What an appropriate name for Dr. Evans. Perhaps the word Amen has lost its power and meaning for us. But in the early church it was a word of power, a word of faith, a word of affirmation, a word of commitment and surrender."

"On behalf of us all, I say Amen!"

Again in 1996, Reverend Moore returned to Dyersburg, Tennessee, to offer the eulogy at Helen Evans' funeral:

"Mrs. Evans was truly a remarkable person. In her own way and in her fulfillment of her accepted role in life, she was as remarkable and unforgettable as Dr. Evans was in his special way. Dr. Evans set the pace and provided the role model for me and my ministry, and Mrs. Evans took Cynthia (his wife) under her wing and guided her in her role as minister's wife. They loved and cared for us and encouraged us from that time on to the present. They treated us as family!"

"Mrs. Evans was remarkable in her willingness to play a supporting role in life. She did not marry a preacher, she married a lawyer. But, when Dr. Evans accepted the call to ministry and gave up his practice of law, she supported that decision and willingly and lovingly made the sacrifices it brought. If we were giving out awards for best supporting roles, Mrs. Evans would certainly be nominated."

He closed by saying, "If Dr. Evans were here and giving direction to this service, I know that he would not want me to omit a reference to Proverbs 31 and to Mrs. Evans' fulfillment of that description of a virtuous woman and a good wife."

When we were young and attended the final sessions of the Memphis Annual Conference, Bishop William T. Watkins would close the sessions by bringing down his gavel and saying, "We are adjourned sine die." Years later we learned that it meant "without a day being set for meeting again."

So it is with the lives of William S. Evans and Helen Mann Evans, their family, and those whose lives were touched by the ministry of William Slaton and Helen Evans.

AMEN!